Pebble® Plus

ICE AGE ANIMALS

Ground Sloths

by Joy Frisch-Schmoll

Consulting Editor: Gail Saunders-Smith, PhD

Content Consultant: Margaret M. Yacobucci, PhD
Education and Outreach Coordinator,
Paleontological Society; Associate Professor,
Department of Geology, Bowling Green State University

CAPSTONE PRESS
a capstone imprint

Pebble Plus is published by Capstone Press,
1710 Roe Crest Drive, North Mankato, Minnesota 56003
www.capstonepub.com

Library of Congress Cataloging-in-Publication Data
Frisch, Joy, author.
Ground sloths / by Joyce Frisch-Schmoll.
pages cm.—(Pebble Plus. Ice Age Animals)
Summary: "Describes the characteristics, food, habitat, behavior, and extinction of ground sloths"—Provided
by publisher.
Audience: Ages 5–8.
Audience: K to grade 3.
Includes bibliographical references and index.
ISBN 978-1-4914-2101-7 (library binding)
ISBN 978-1-4914-2319-6 (pbk.)
ISBN 978-1-4914-2342-4 (ebook pdf)
1. Ground sloths--Juvenile literature. 2. Extinct mammals—Juvenile literature. I. Title.
QE882.E2F75 2015
569.31—dc23   2014028917

Editorial Credits
Jeni Wittrock, editor; Peggie Carley and Janet Kusmierski, designers; Wanda Winch, media researcher; Laura
Manthe, production specialist

Photo Credits
Illustrator: Jon Hughes
Shutterstock: Alex Staroseltsev, snowball, April Cat, icicles, Leigh Prather, ice crystals, LilKar, cover
background, pcruciatti, interior background

Note to Parents and Teachers

The Ice Age Animals set supports national science standards related to life science.
This book describes and illustrates ground sloths. The images support early readers in
understanding the text. The repetition of words and phrases helps early readers learn
new words. This book also introduces early readers to subject-specific vocabulary words,
which are defined in the Glossary section. Early readers may need assistance to read
some words and to use the Table of Contents, Glossary, Read More, Internet Sites, and
Index sections of the book.

Printed in China by Nordica.
0914/CA21401504
092014   008470NORDS15

Table of Contents

A Strange Beast 4

Ground Level 8

Big and Strong 12

Gentle Giants 16

Glossary 22

Read More 23

Internet Sites 23

Index 24

A Strange Beast

Slow, heavy footsteps move
through the forest. Crack!
Giant claws break a branch.
A big ground sloth chomps
on the leaves.

About 35,000 years ago,
ground sloths roamed the land.
Some were the size of black
bears. Others were as big
as elephants!

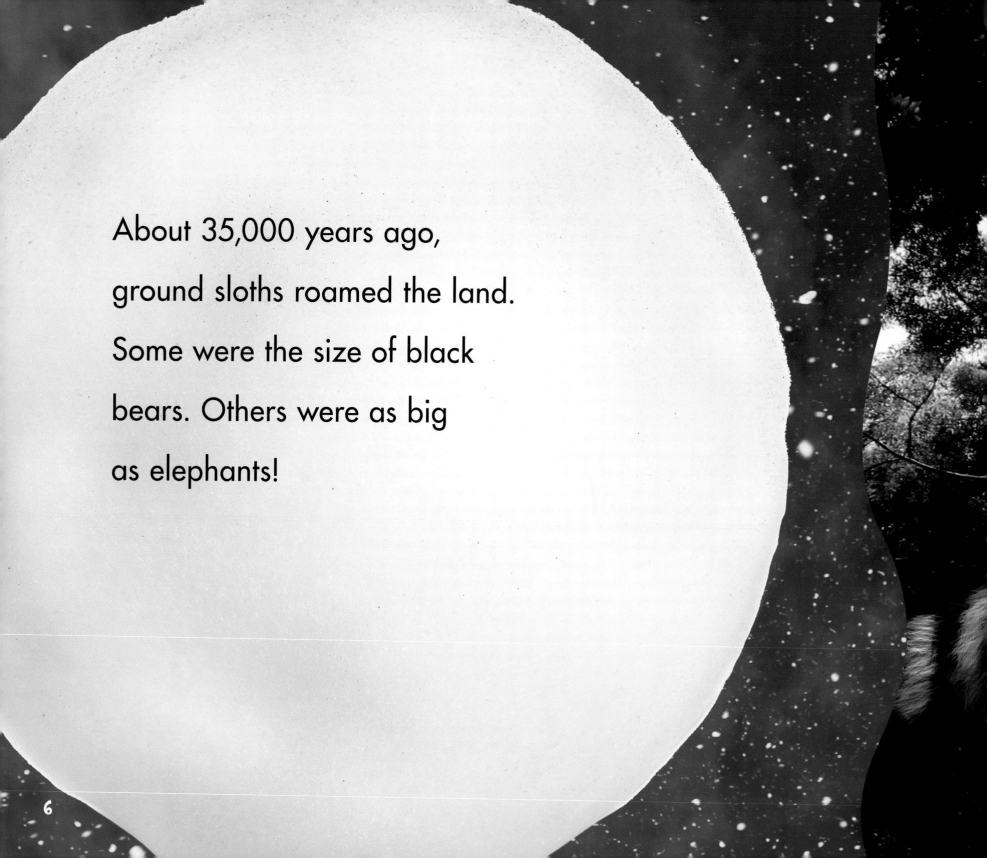

Ground Level

Ground sloths lived in North and South America during the Ice Age. They made their homes in caves, grasslands, and forests.

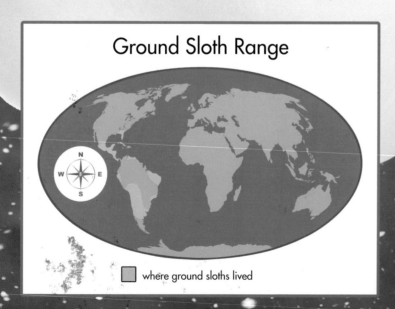

Ground Sloth Range

where ground sloths lived

Too big to climb trees, ground sloths lived on the ground. They walked on all fours with their clawed feet turned in.

Big and Strong

Ground sloths had shaggy fur and sharp claws. They stood on strong back legs to reach the leafy treetops. Thick tails helped them balance.

Along with leaves, sloths ate twigs and grasses. Their powerful jaws and flat teeth were good for grinding up plants.

Gentle Giants

Ground sloths lived on their own. Sloths were slow and gentle. But if a sloth was attacked, it would fight back.

A fighting ground sloth
stood up to look bigger.
Swipe! It swung its front
claws at predators, such
as the sabertooth cat.

About 10,000 years ago, Earth changed. The planet warmed. Human hunters moved in. With less food and more predators, ground sloths became extinct.

Glossary

claw—a hard, curved nail on the foot of an animal

extinct—no longer living; an extinct animal is one that has died out, with no more of its kind

grassland—a large, open area where grass and low plants grow

Ice Age—a time when much of Earth was covered in ice; the last ice age ended about 11,500 years ago

jaw—the part of the mouth used to grab, bite, and chew

predator—an animal that hunts other animals for food

Read More

Higgins, Melissa. *Woolly Mammoths.* Ice Age Animals. North Mankato, Minn.: Capstone Press, 2015.

Laverdunt, Damien. *Small and Tall Tales of Extinct Animals.* Gecko Press Titles. Minneapolis: Lerner Pub., 2012.

Zabludoff, Marc. *Giant Ground Sloth.* Tarrytown, N.Y.: Marshall Cavendish Benchmark, 2010.

Internet Sites

FactHound offers a safe, fun way to find Internet sites related to this book. All of the sites on FactHound have been researched by our staff.

Here's all you do:

Visit *www.facthound.com*

Type in this code: 9781491421017

Check out projects, games and lots more at
www.capstonekids.com

Index

attacks, 16, 18
caves, 8
claws, 4, 10, 12, 18
extinct, 20
feet, 4, 10
fighting, 18
food, 4, 14, 20
forests, 4, 8
fur, 12,
gentle, 16
grasslands, 8
homes, 8
humans, 20

hunters, 20
jaws, 14
leaves, 4, 12, 14
predators, 18, 20
size, 4, 6, 10, 18
speed, 16
standing, 12, 18
tails, 12
teeth, 14
walking, 10
warming, 20

Word Count: 196
Grade: 1
Early-Intervention Level: 18